Project 7-11

CW01667289

Back to Basics

MATHS

for 8-9 year olds

George Rodda

Letts

Addition

Hundreds **T**ens **U**nits

H	T	U
1	8	7
3	5	4
5	4	1

$7 + 4 = 11$

$80 + 50 = 130$

$100 + 300 = 400 +$

541

Finish these additions.

1 264 + 325 = ___9

2 372 + 428 = ___0

3 482 + 284 = ____

4 111 + 456 = ____

5 293 + 371 = ____

6 350 + 305 = ____

7 586 + 16 = ____

8 586 + 106 = ____

9 399 + 399 = ____

10 500 + 500 = ____

11 409 + 904 = ____

12 499 + 501 = ____

13 Add 239 and 932.

14 Find the total of 393 and 939.

15 What is the sum of 999 and 1? ______

16 What is the sum of 999 and 100? ______

Reflections

Draw the reflection to complete the pictures.

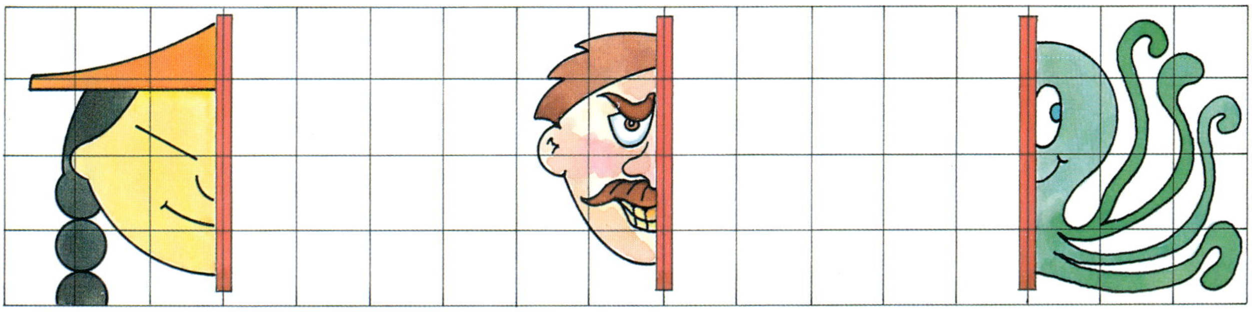

Draw the reflection and complete the name of the shape.

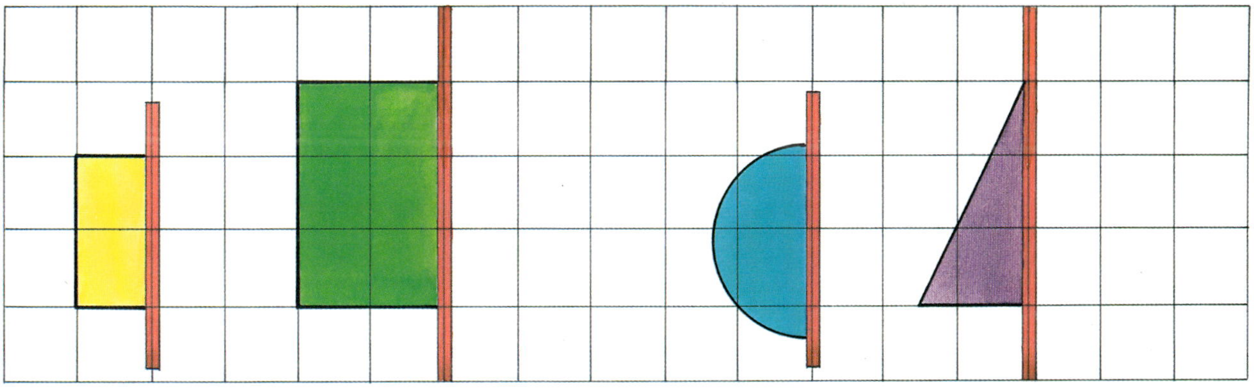

squ ____________ re ______________ ci ______________ tr ______________

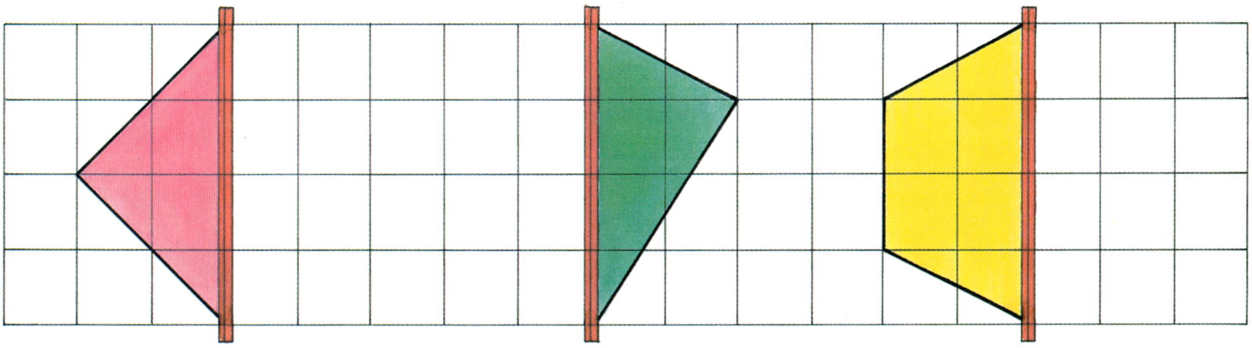

s ______________________ k ______________________ h ______________________

Points from numbers

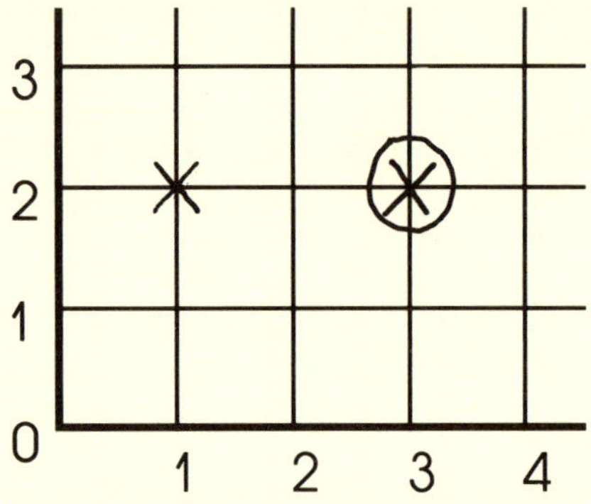

X marks the point (1,2)

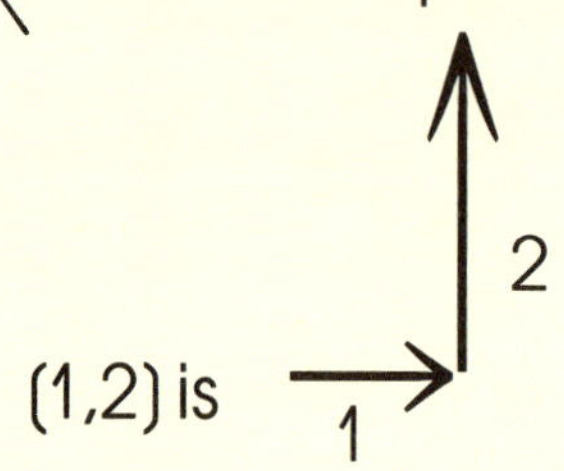

(X) marks the point (3,2)

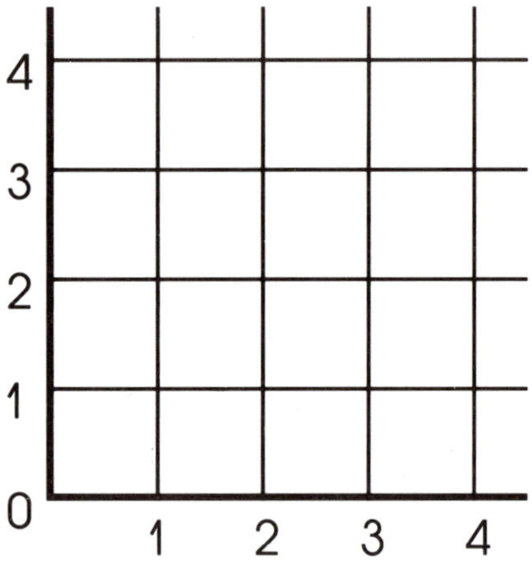

Mark these points with **X**.

(1,1), (3,1), (3,3), (1,3)

Join the points in the order

(1,1) → (3,1) → (3,3) → (1,3) → (1,1)

What is the name of the shape

you have drawn? ____________________

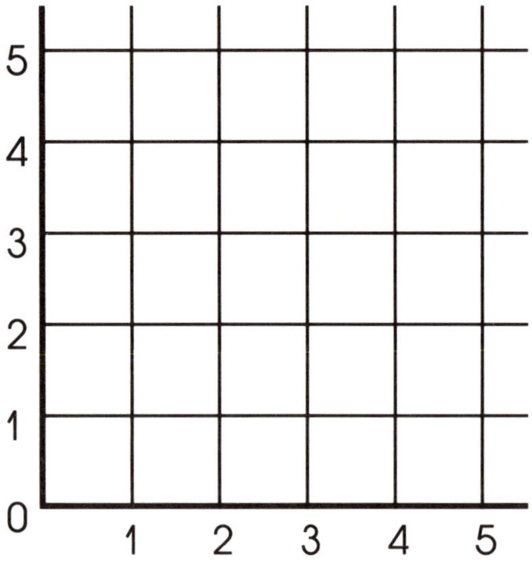

Mark these points with **X**.

(0,4), (4,4), (4,1), (0,1)

Join the points in the order

(0,4) → (4,4) → (4,1) → (0,1) → (0,4)

What is the name of the shape

you have drawn? ____________________

Use the squares to help you answer these questions.

Which point makes a square with (2,2), (2,4) and (4,4)? (__ , __)

Which point makes a square with (2,2), (1,4) and (3,5)? (__ , __)

Fifty pence

A 50p coin can be exchanged for two 20p coins and one 10p coin.

(50p) → 2 (20p) and 1 (10p)

Write in the missing numbers and coin values.

1 (50p) → 5 (p)

2 (50p) → [ ] (5p)

3 (50p) → 50 (p)

4 (50p) → [ ] (2p)

5 (50p) → (10p) + [ ] (20p)

6 (50p) → (20p) + [ ] (10p)

7 (50p) → (10p) + [ ] (5p)

8 (50p) → (10p) + [ ] (2p)

9 (50p) → [ ] (20p) + 2 (5p)

10 (50p) → [ ] (5p) + 5 (2p)

11

[ ]p
+ 17p
50p

12

£ [ ]
+ £0.23
£0.50

13

£0.39
+£ [ ]
£0.50

14

42p
+ [ ]p
50p

15 How many 50p coins make £5? [ ]

16 Are two 50p coins equal in value to fifty 2p coins?

____

Squares and rectangles

This is part of a shop window display.

How many tins of beans are there on display? ________

How many boxes of cornflakes are there on display? ________

Arrange **12 tins** of beans in these rectangular displays.

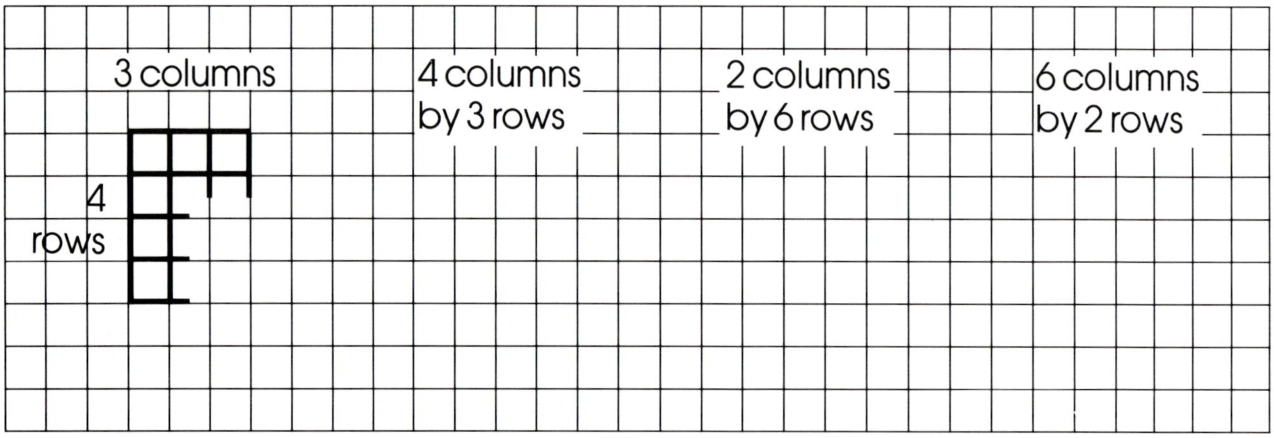

Draw oranges to show these numbers in square displays.

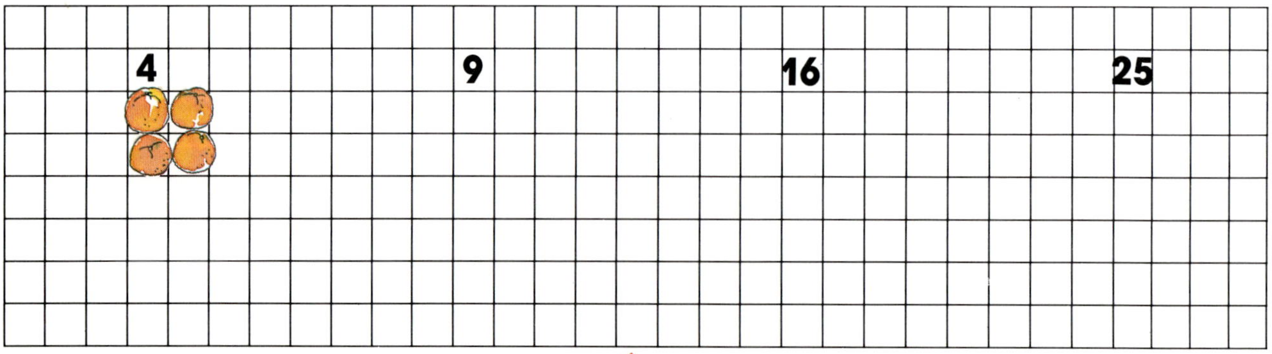

Take away

$$\begin{array}{r} 323 \\ -\,104 \\ \hline 219 \\ \hline \end{array}$$

The sunflower is 219 cm taller than the daffodil.

Complete these subtractions.

1 $\begin{array}{r} 173 \\ -\ \ 62 \\ \hline \\ \hline \end{array}$ **2** $\begin{array}{r} 458 \\ -347 \\ \hline \\ \hline \end{array}$ **3** $\begin{array}{r} 343 \\ -124 \\ \hline \\ \hline \end{array}$ **4** $\begin{array}{r} 856 \\ -666 \\ \hline \\ \hline \end{array}$

5 $\begin{array}{r} 743 \\ -\ \ 54 \\ \hline \\ \hline \end{array}$ **6** $\begin{array}{r} 642 \\ -\ \ 99 \\ \hline \\ \hline \end{array}$ **7** $\begin{array}{r} 999 \\ -827 \\ \hline \\ \hline \end{array}$ **8** $\begin{array}{r} 444 \\ -345 \\ \hline \\ \hline \end{array}$

9 $\begin{array}{r} 1000 \\ -\ \ 100 \\ \hline \\ \hline \end{array}$ **10** $\begin{array}{r} 1000 \\ -\ \ \ \ 99 \\ \hline \\ \hline \end{array}$ **11** $\begin{array}{r} 1010 \\ -\ \ 101 \\ \hline \\ \hline \end{array}$ **12** $\begin{array}{r} 1000 \\ -\ \ 888 \\ \hline \\ \hline \end{array}$

13 Write down the number which is 1 less than 1000. ______________

14 Write down the number which is 10 less than 1000. ______________

Fill in the missing numbers.

15 $\begin{array}{r} 357 \\ -\ \ 76 \\ \hline 2\_1 \\ \hline \end{array}$ **16** $\begin{array}{r} 3\_0\_ \\ -1999 \\ \hline 1001 \\ \hline \end{array}$ **17** $\begin{array}{r} 274 \\ -\_3\_ \\ \hline 142 \\ \hline \end{array}$ **18** $\begin{array}{r} 572 \\ -\_44 \\ \hline 3\_8 \\ \hline \end{array}$

Right angles

The corner of this book is a **right angle**

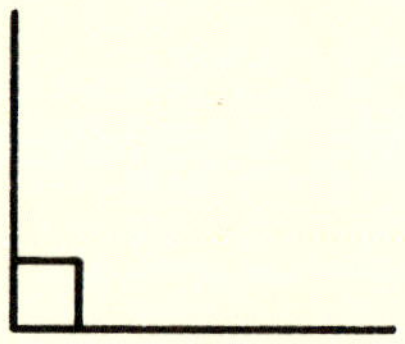

1 right angle

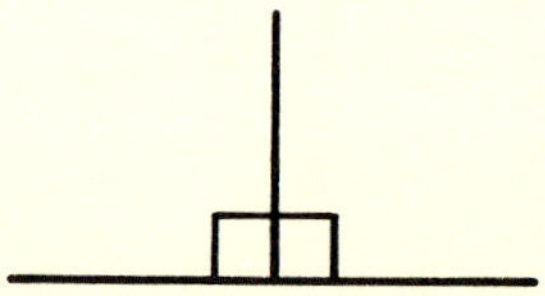

2 right angles

Mark each angle which is a right angle.

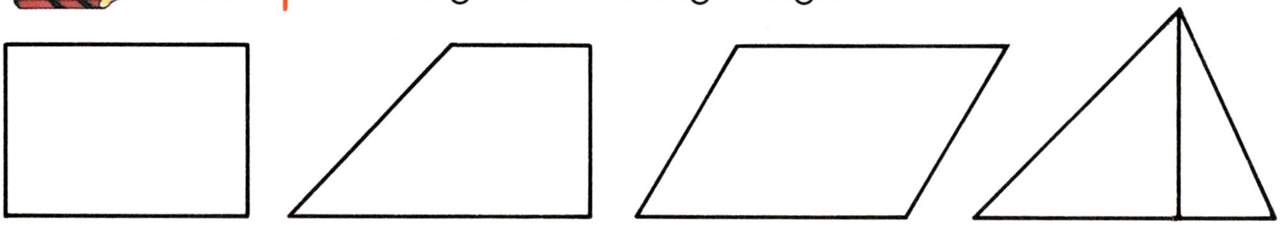

Mark angles which are less than a right angle.

Fill in the missing flag numbers.

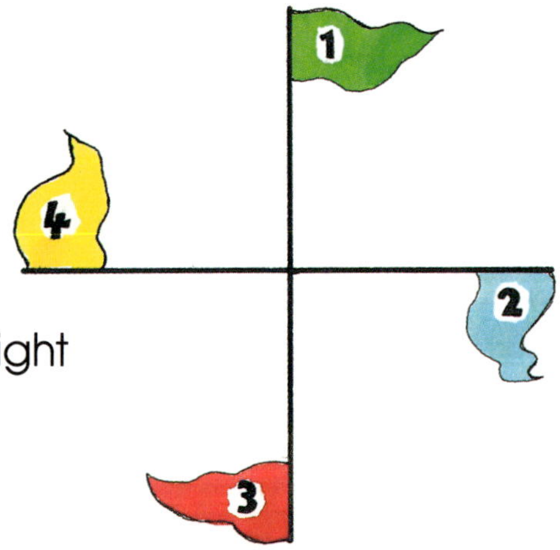

When flag 1 is turned clockwise through one right angle it becomes flag number

_________.

When flag 4 is turned anti-clockwise through one right angle it becomes flag number

_________.

When flag 1 is turned anti-clockwise through 2 right angles it will become flag number

_________.

Addition squares

400	20	4	424
300	60	5	365
700	80	9	789

424 ← 400 + 20 + 4

365 ← 300 + 60 + 5

789 ← 424 + 365 and 700 + 80 + 9

400 + 300 → 700

20 + 60 → 80

4 + 5 → 9

Complete these addition squares.

1

300	40	3	
200	20	5	
			568

2

500	40	7	
200	30	3	

3

400	50	4	
400	30	5	

4

500	40	7	
200	30	2	

5

200	40	5	
300	20	3	

6

200	20	2	
600	60	8	

7

300	40	5	
300	40	5	

8

400	30	6	
300	50	5	

9

200	70	3	
500	30	4	

10

100	50	4	
200	50	4	

11

400	90	5	
300	10	5	

12

400	90	2	
300	10	5	

Thousands

This bank was built in the year 1893.

1893 is one thousand eight hundred and ninety three.

Write these numbers in figures.

1 three thousand four hundred and thirty two ______

2 one thousand two hundred and twenty ______

3 two thousand and forty one ______

4 one thousand and twenty ______

Finish these sums.

5 1324 + 2135	**6** 2463 + 624	**7** 1553 + 452	**8** 357 + 643
9 2457 + 1407	**10** 3541 + 1152	**11** 2653 + 732	**12** 3524 + 1536

Use these spaces to work out:

13 927 + 323 + 1005

14 666 + 777 + 888

13 +

14 +

Digital time

The clock and the watch show 2 minutes past 3.

2 minutes past 3 is the same time as 3.02.

Show these times in the way the watch shows time.

1 6 minutes past 3

2 10 minutes past 3

3 15 minutes past 3

4 15 min. past 10

5 15 min. past 11

6 25 past 9

7 ½ past 9

8 25 minutes to 10

9 20 to 10

10 5 min. to 9

11 1 min. to 12

12 11 min. past 11

13 An early morning video starts at 15 minutes past 7 and lasts for 90 minutes. Show the

starting time   and finishing time

14 My radio alarm needs setting for 10 minutes to 7. Put the numbers in.

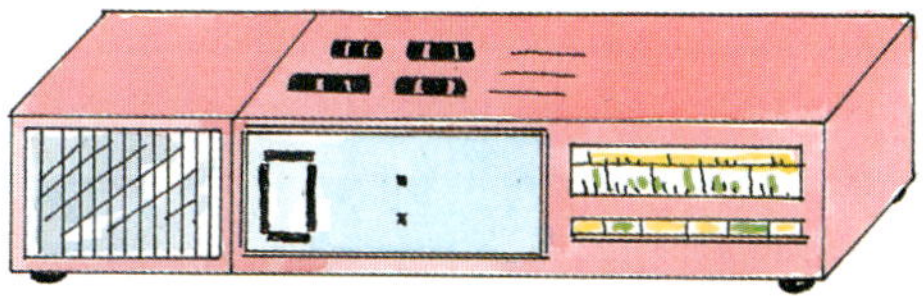

15 Set this alarm for the time you need to get up for your school morning.

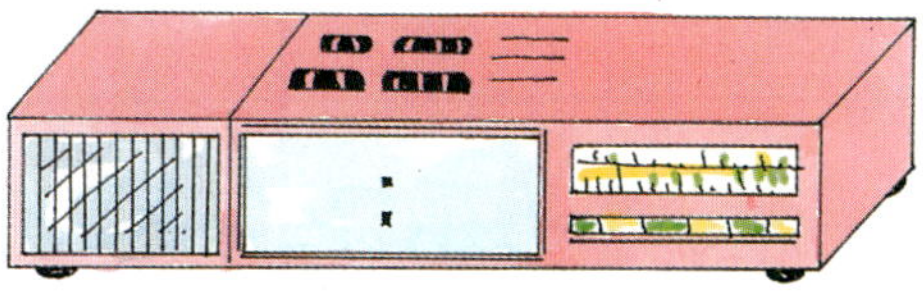

Total value

1 of 50p + 1 of 20p + 2 of 10p + 3 of 2p

50p + 20p + 20p + 6p = 96p

Fill in the totals.

Coins						
50p	20p	10p	5p	2p	1p	Total value
	1	4	2		3	73p
	1	1	1	1	1	
	2		2	2	2	
1		1		1		
	2	2	2	2	2	
	3		3		3	
1	2		1	2		
	2	2	2		7	
			9	9	9	
			10	10	10	
		5	5		5	
1	1	1	1			
1	2	3	4	5		
2	3	4	5			

Tallying

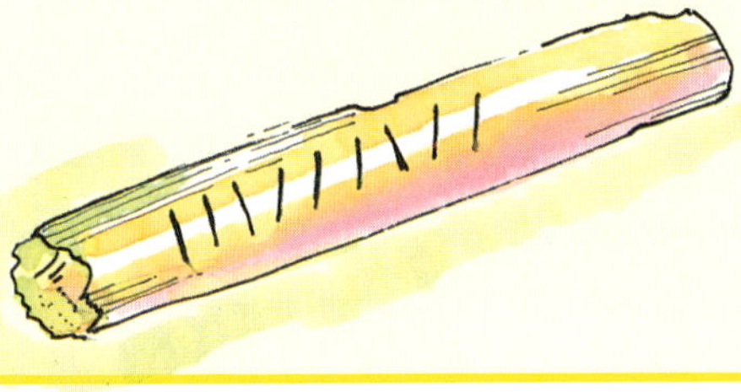

This is a tally stick.

It has 𝍸 IIII notches on it.

↑ ↑

5 + 4 = 9 notches

Each mark I represents one child in Class 2.
Finish the tally and write in the number of children.

Age		Tally	Number
7 years	IIIIIII	𝍸 II	7
8 years	IIIIIIIIIIII		
9 years	IIIIIIIII		

Finish drawing this graph which shows the number of children for each age in Class 2.

Each mark represents a pet.
Fill in the tally and number.

		Tally	Number
Dog	IIIIIIII		
Cat	IIIIIII		
Fish	IIII		

Draw a graph showing the number of each pet.

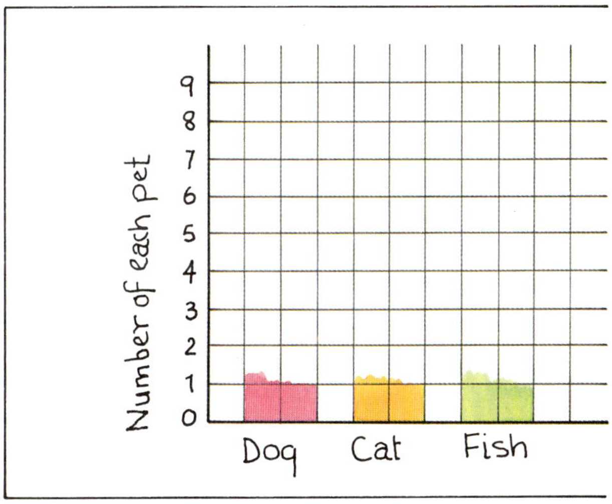

Multiplication tables

×	5	6	7
5	25	30	35
6	30	36	42

$5 \times 7 = 35$

$6 \times 5 = 30$

Fill in these tables.

×	3	4	5
5			25
6			30

×	4	5	6
7			
8			

×	7	8	9
5	35		
6	42		

×	7	8
4		
6		
8		

×	7	8
3		
5		
7		

×	4	5
5		
7		
9		

×	4	5
6		
8		
10		

×	5	7	9
5			
7			
9			

×	4	6	8
4			
6			
8			

×	0	5	10
0			
5			
10			

×	1	2	3	4	5
5					
6					
7					

×	6	7	8	9	10
5					
6					
7					

A calendar month

This is a page from a calendar.

Mon	–	6	13	20	27
Tues	–	7	14	21	28
Wed	1	8	15	22	–
Thurs	2	9	16	23	–
Fri	3	10	17	24	–
Sat	4	11	18	25	–
Sun	5	12	19	26	–

For the month:

1 How many days are there in the month? ________

2 How many weeks are there in the month? ________

3 Which month is the page for? ________________

4 How many even numbered days are there? ________

5 How many odd numbered days are there? ________

6 In what kind of year does this month have one day more?

____

This is the calendar page for the same month in a different year.

7 Finish totalling the rows.

8 Finish totalling the columns.

9 Put a red cross on each multiple of 2.

10 Put a blue circle round each multiple of 3.

						Totals
Mon	1	8	15	22	–	
Tues	2	9	16	23	–	50
Wed	3	10	17	24	–	
Thurs	4	11	18	25	–	
Fri	5	12	19	26	–	
Sat	6	13	20	27	–	
Sun	7	14	21	28	–	
Totals				175	0	

Money

Using as few coins as possible
19p can be paid with

1 of 10p, 1 of 5p and 2 of 2p.

Fill in this table to make up the amount using as few coins as possible.

	Coins to use:					
	50p	20p	10p	5p	2p	1p
Make up: 16p	—	—	1			
35p						
19p	—	—	1	1	2	—
49p						
59p						
28p						
63p						
77p						
79p						
84p						
98p						
99p						
£1						

Time

This clock shows 15 minutes past 7

or 7.15.

a.m. is time **before** midday

p.m. is time **after** midday

This clock shows ½ past 1.

What time will it be in:

1 10 minutes?

_______ to _______

2 20 minutes?

_______ to _______

3 30 minutes?

____

4 5 minutes?

____

5 25 minutes?

____

6 1 hour?

____

7 45 minutes?

____

8 50 minutes?

____

This clock shows my breakfast time.

It is 20 past 8 or 8.20 a.m.

What time will it be in:

9 2 hours?

___________ a.m.

10 6 hours?

___________ p.m.

11 5 hours?

___________ p.m.

12 1½ hours?

___________ a.m.

13 5¼ hours?

___________ p.m.

14 12½ hours?

___________ p.m.

Dividing (1)

A gardener planted 21 rose bushes in rows of 5.

21 ÷ 5 = 4 remainder 1.

Make more marks / to group these cars in threes.

The cars can be divided into _____ groups of 3 with _____ remainder.

Write down the answers.

1	24 ÷ 2 = ___	**2**	24 ÷ 3 = ___	**3**	24 ÷ 6 = ___	**4**	24 ÷ 8 = ___
5	39 ÷ 3 = ___	**6**	45 ÷ 5 = ___	**7**	35 ÷ 7 = ___	**8**	42 ÷ 6 = ___
9	68 ÷ 4 = ___	**10**	80 ÷ 8 = ___	**11**	72 ÷ 8 = ___	**12**	81 ÷ 9 = ___
13	72 ÷ 6 = ___	**14**	99 ÷ 9 = ___	**15**	85 ÷ 5 = ___	**16**	77 ÷ 7 = ___

Write the answers and the remainders.

1	15 ÷ 4 = _____ rem _____	**2**	23 ÷ 2 = _____ rem _____
3	33 ÷ 2 = _____ rem _____	**4**	31 ÷ 5 = _____ rem _____
5	16 ÷ 3 = _____ rem _____	**6**	43 ÷ 4 = _____ rem _____
7	37 ÷ 6 = _____ rem _____	**8**	53 ÷ 6 = _____ rem _____
9	50 ÷ 7 = _____ rem _____	**10**	91 ÷ 9 = _____ rem _____

Twenty chocolates are shared by 4 children.

How many do they have each? __________

Bar graphs

Here is a graph of the number of

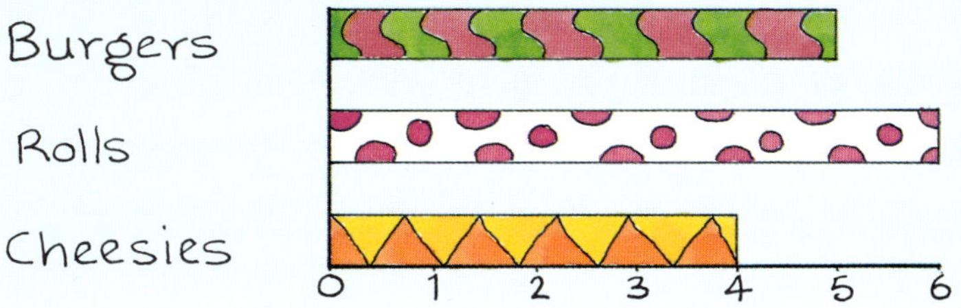

bought by Ian.

Fill in the missing numbers.

Ian bought _____ burgers, _____ rolls and _____ cheesies.

On this grid draw a graph showing the number of pupils absent each day.

	Mon	Tues	Wed	Thurs	Fri
Absent	10	6	7	4	9

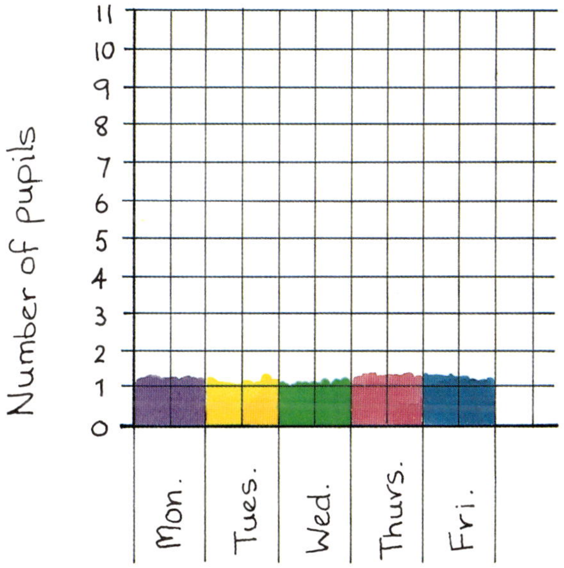

Which day had the worst attendance? ____________________

Which day had the best attendance? ____________________

This graph shows a count of traffic passing a school.

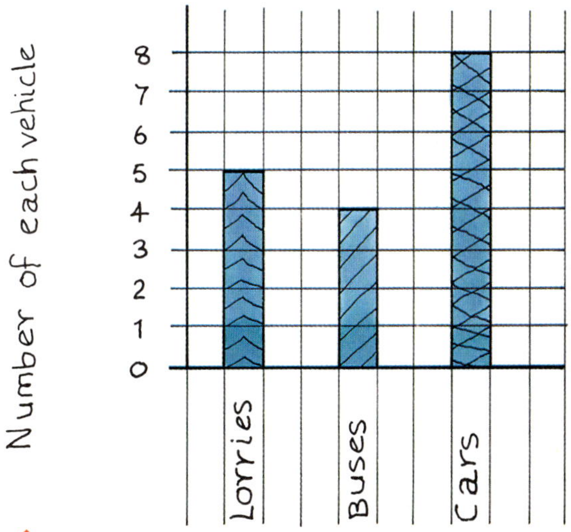

How many of each vehicle passed the school?

Cars _____ Lorries _____ Buses _____

What was the total number?

____

Sums from words

I counted 8 cars
with 4 wheels each.

There are 8×4
$= 32$ wheels.

Write the sum and find the answer.

1 I counted 15 bicycles and then 4 more. $15 + 4$

How many bicycles were there? $= \square$

2 Peter counted 15 rabbits in a cage. $\square \times \square$

How many legs did they have altogether? $= \square$

3 30 eggs were packed 6 to a box. $30 \quad \square$

How many boxes were needed? $= \square$

4 A shelf had 57 books on it.
I took 29 books away.
How many books were left? $\square \quad \square$ $= \square$

5 Chocolates are packed in boxes of 10. $\square \quad \square$

How many chocolates fill five boxes? $= \square$

6 60 sheep have to be put into 5 pens.
How many will there be in each pen? $\square$

7 9 bars of chocolate are each broken into 8 pieces.
How many pieces are there? $\square$

8 My film will take 36 photographs. I have taken 19, how many more can I take? $\square$

Multiplication (1)

4	2	8
3	1	3
12	2	24

Row 1: $4 \times 2 = 8$

Row 2: $3 \times 1 = 3$

Row 3: $8 \times 3 = 24$ and 12×2

Column 1: 4×3

Column 2: 2×1

Finish these multiplication squares.

1

3	2	
1	4	
		24

2

1	2	
3	4	

3

2	3	
4	4	

4

2	4	
3	5	

5

1	7	
2	4	

6

3	8	
4	0	

Complete these multiplications.

7 43×4 = ___

8 43×5 = ___

9 34×3 = ___

10 49×2 = ___

11 67×7 = ___

12 49×6 = ___

13 75×8 = ___

14 33×9 = ___

15 $40 \times 10 =$ ______

16 $41 \times 10 =$ ______

Dividing (2)

Mary has worked out these divisions.

$27 \div 3 = 9$ ✓

$28 \div 3 = 9$ rem 1 ✓

$270 \div 3 = 90$ ✓

$269 \div 3 = 89$ rem 2 ✓

Work these out.

1 $30 \div 3 =$ ____

2 $33 \div 3 =$ ____

3 $330 \div 3 =$ ____

4 $333 \div 3 =$ ____

5 $25 \div 5 =$ ____

6 $175 \div 5 =$ ____

7 $240 \div 4 =$ ____

8 $240 \div 3 =$ ____

9 $178 \div 2 =$ ____

10 $188 \div 4 =$ ____

11 $690 \div 2 =$ ____

12 $688 \div 4 =$ ____

Complete these divisions which have remainders.

13 $34 \div 3 =$ ____ rem 1

14 $340 \div 3 =$ ____ rem ____

15 $344 \div 3 =$ ____ rem ____

16 $34 \div 4 =$ ____ rem ____

17 $267 \div 5 =$ ____ rem ____

18 $563 \div 2 =$ ____ rem ____

19 $106 \div 4 =$ ____ rem ____

20 $705 \div 5 =$ ____ rem ____

21 Which is the greater $72 \div 2$ or $72 \div 4$? ____

22 Which is the greater $72 \div 6$ or $72 \div 3$? ____

23 Divide 2632 by 2. ____

24 Divide 2632 by 1. ____

mm and cm

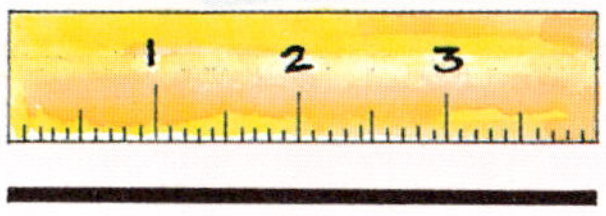

4 cm
or 40 mm

This line is 4 cm long.

1 cm = 10 mm

so 4 cm = 40 mm

How long is the side of this square in mm?

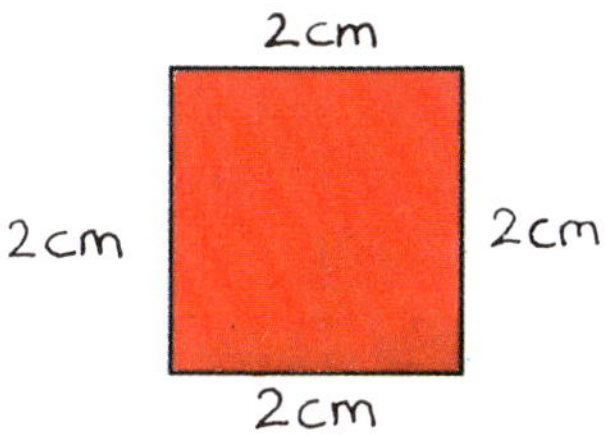

_____ mm

How far is it round the edge of the square in cm?

_____ cm,

= _____ mm.

Fill in the missing numbers for this triangle.

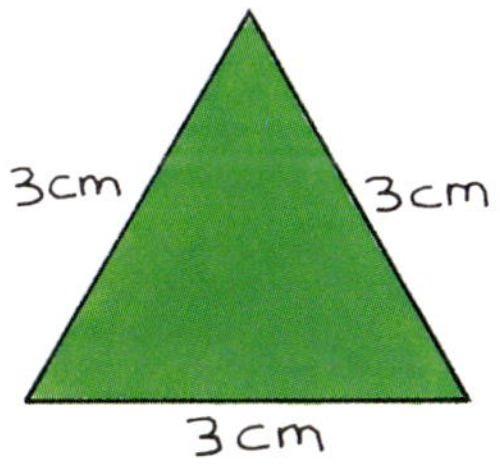

The length of one edge is _____ cm,

= _____ mm.

The distance all the way round the triangle is

_____ cm,

= _____ mm.

Fill in the missing numbers for this rectangle.

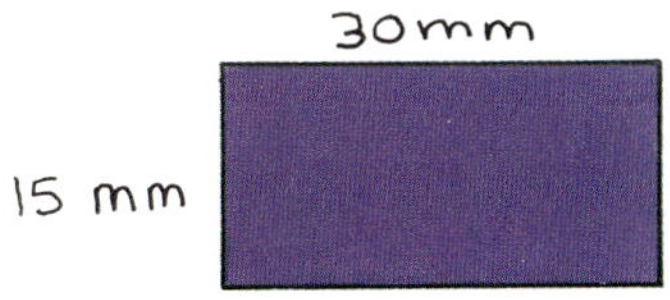

The length of the long side is _____ cm.

The length of the short side is _____ cm.

The distance all the way round is _____ mm

or _____ cm.

Cubes

This block is **3** cubes long,

2 cubes wide

and **2** cubes high.

There are **6** cubes on each layer.

There are $2 \times 6 = 12$ cubes in this block.

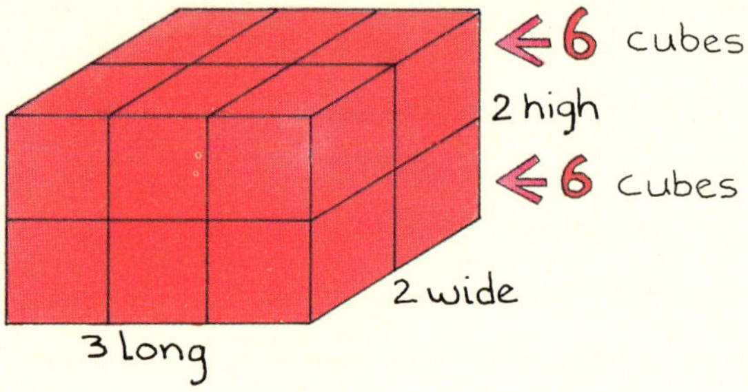

Write down the number of cubes in these blocks.

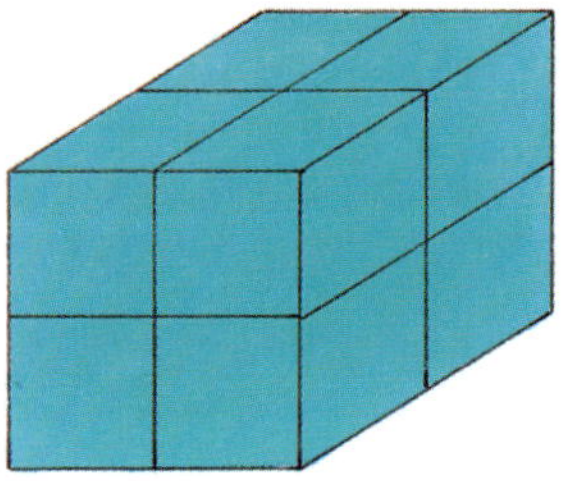

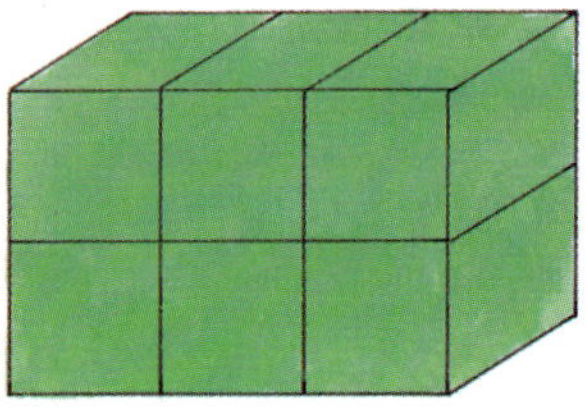

Number of cubes

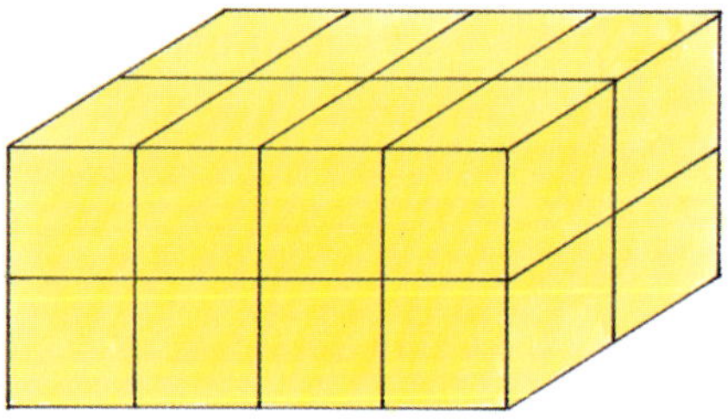

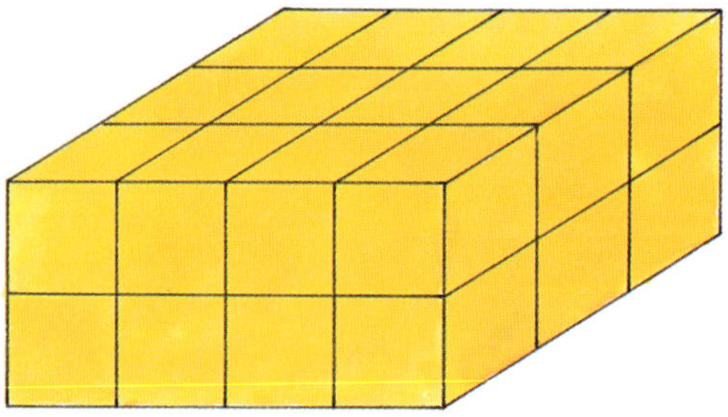

12 cubes can be arranged in different ways.

Fill in the numbers for these different blocks using 12 cubes.

Long	3	3	2	6	6	2
Wide	2	4	2	2	1	1
High	2	1				

Weight

These items are weighed in grammes. (g)

Write in **more than** or **less than**.

1 A Rollo weighs ________________ a Minty Log.

2 A Rollo weighs ________________ a Choco.

3 A Toffee Slab weighs ________________ a Minty Log.

4 A Choco weighs ________________ a Toffee Slab.

5 Two Rollos weigh ________________ a Toffee Slab.

Write in the weights and find the total weight.

1 Choco		g	2 Rollos		g	3 Logs		g
1 Rollo		g	1 Toffee		g	2 Rollos		g
2 Logs	200	g	1 Choco		g	1 Choco		g
Total		g	Total		g	Total		g

1 Choco		g	2 Chocos		g	½ Choco		g
1 Rollo		g	2 Rollos		g	½ Rollo		g
1 Log		g	2 Logs		g	½ Log		g
1 Toffee		g	2 Toffees		g	½ Toffee		g
Total		g	Total		g	Total		g

Grammes and kilogrammes

This bag of sugar and the bag of peas weigh the same.

1000 g = 1 kg

Complete these sums.

1
  300g
+700g
_____
_____

2
  250g
+750g
_____
_____

3
  1065g
– 445g
_____
_____

4
  2000g
– 650g
_____
_____

5 100g × 10

= ☐ g = ☐ kg

6 50g × 20

= ☐ g = ☐ kg

7 100g × 20

= ☐ g = ☐ kg

8 20g × 100

= ☐ g = ☐ kg

Write down the number of grammes.

9 $\frac{1}{2}$ kg = _____ g

10 $\frac{1}{4}$ kg = _____ g

11 $\frac{1}{10}$ kg = _____ g

12 $\frac{3}{10}$ kg = _____ g

Find the total weight on each plate.

A

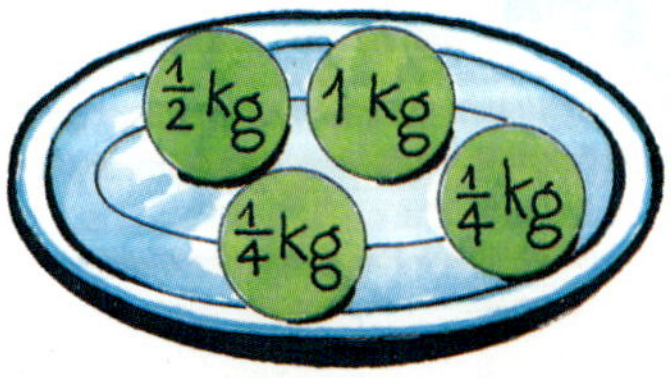

B

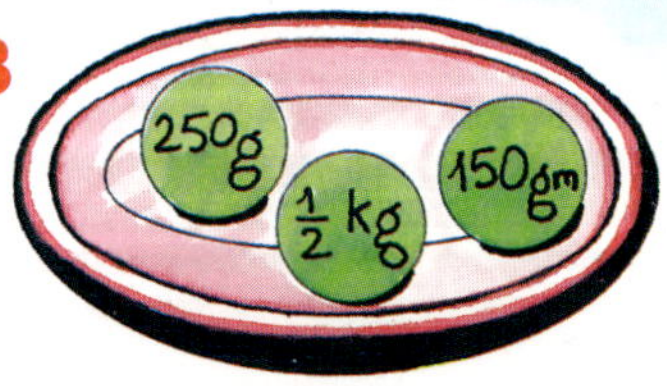

C

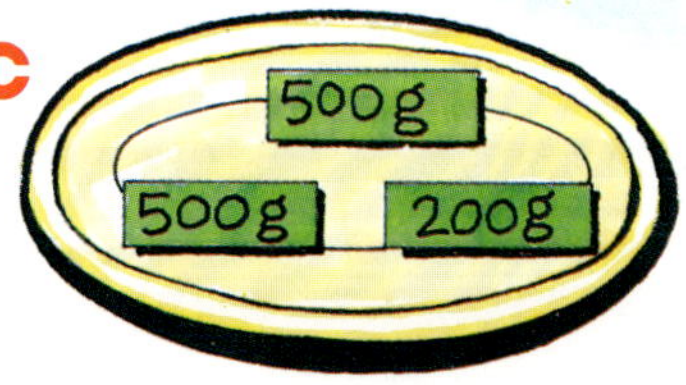

Total weight **A** _____ g **B** _____ g **C** _____ g

Which plate is the lightest, **A**, **B**, or **C**? _____

Fractions (1)

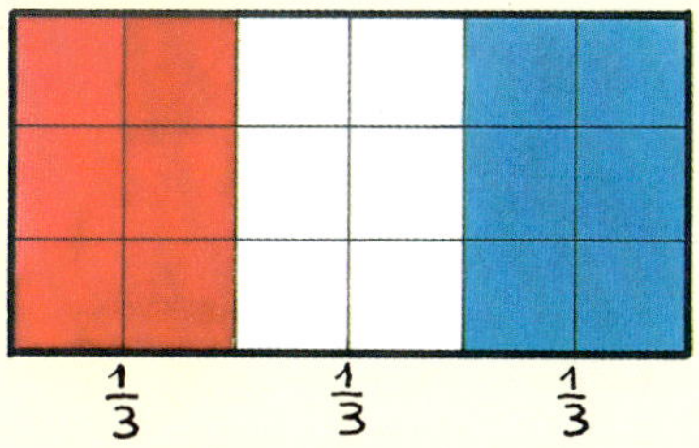

⅓ of this flag is red,

⅓ is white

and ⅓ is blue.

Fill in these fractions.

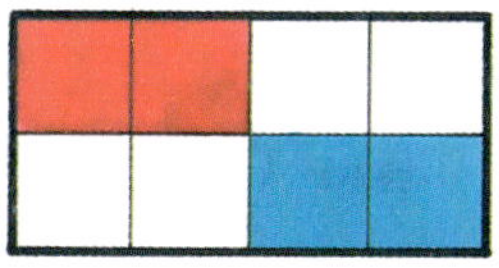

________ is red
________ is white
________ is blue

________ is red
________ is white
________ is blue

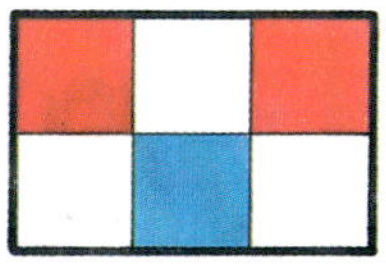

________ is red
________ is white
________ is blue

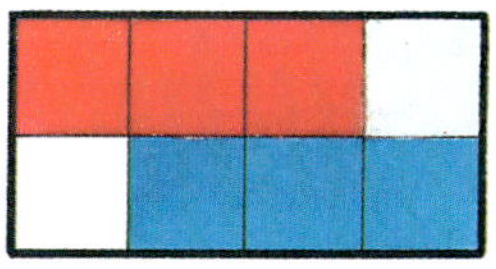

________ is red
________ is white
________ is blue

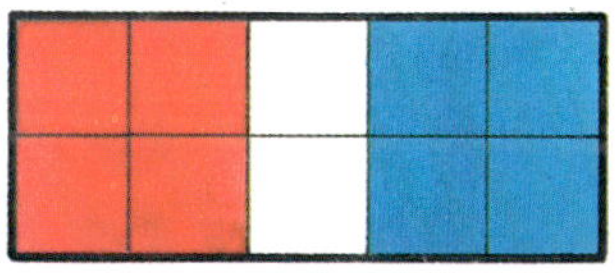

________ is red
________ is white
________ is blue

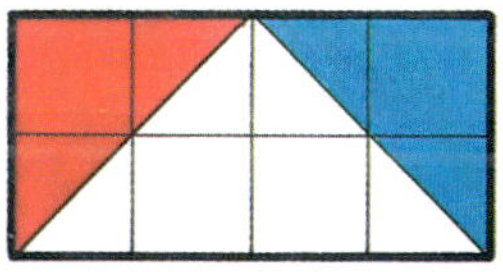

________ is red
________ is white
________ is blue

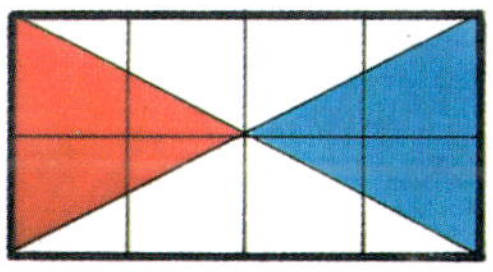

________ is red
________ is white
________ is blue

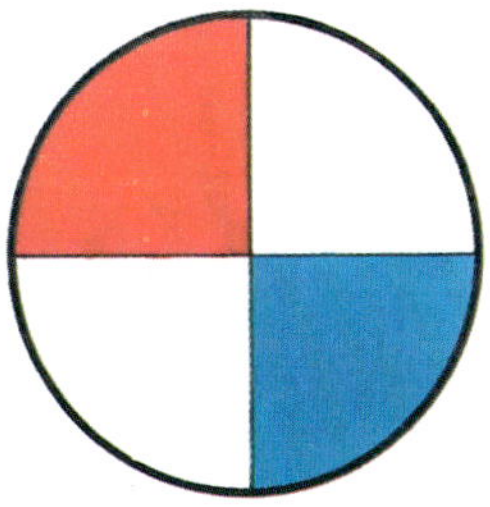

________ is red
________ is white
________ is blue

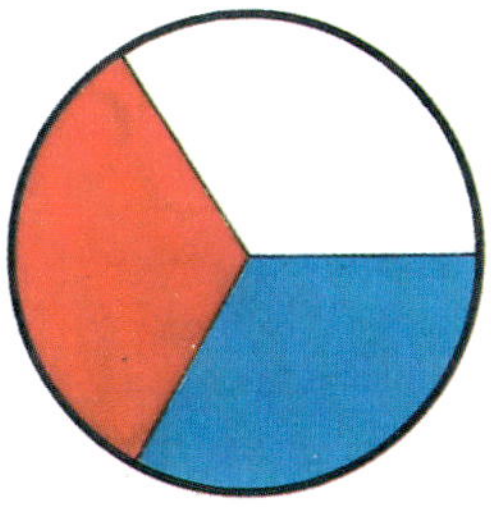

________ is red
________ is white
________ is blue

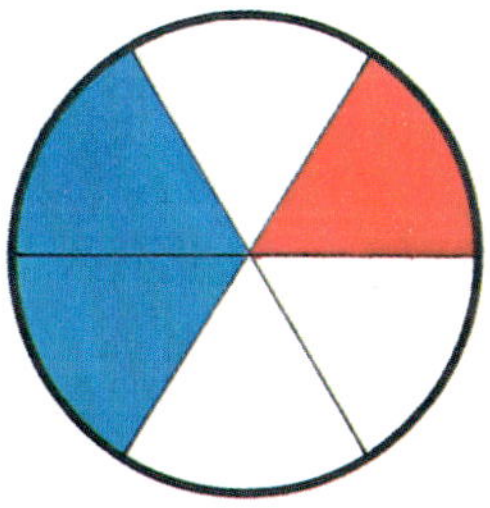

________ is red
________ is white
________ is blue

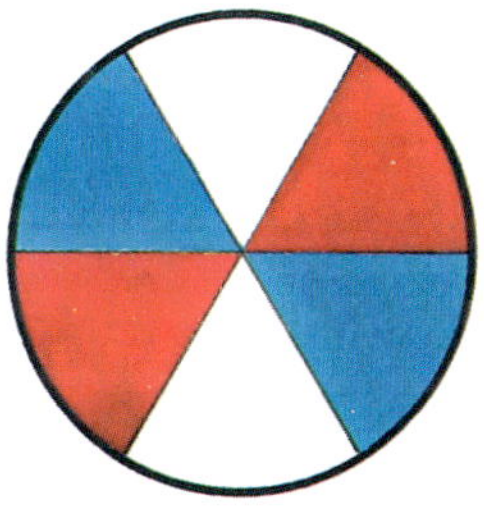

________ is red
________ is white
________ is blue

Length (1)

A foot is an old measure of length.

This hairy foot is 25cm long.

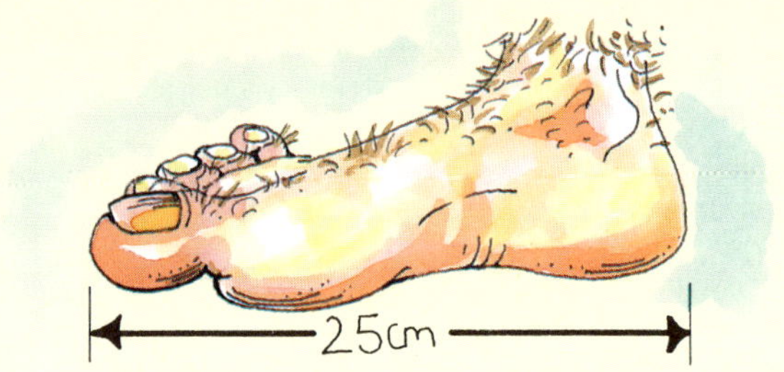

Fill in the table for hairy feet.

Hairy feet	1	2	3	4	5
Total length	25 cm	cm	cm	cm	cm

Hairy feet	10	20	30	40
Total length	2 m 50 cm	m	m cm	m

How many hairy feet will just fit round these squares?

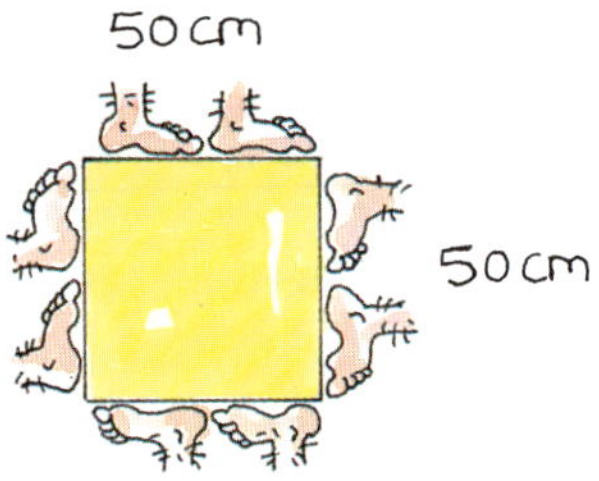

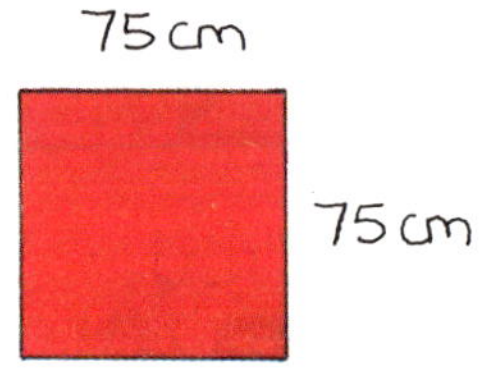

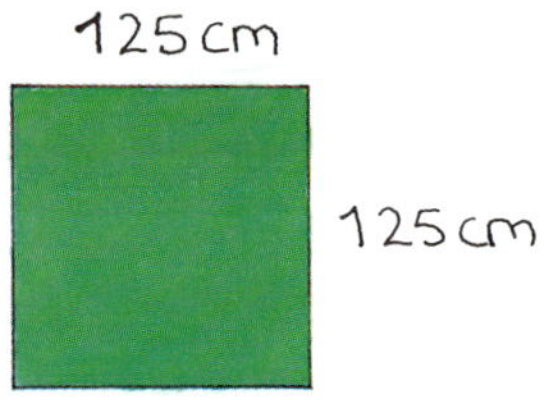

_______ hairy feet   _______ hairy feet   _______ hairy feet

How many hairy feet will just fit round these rectangles?

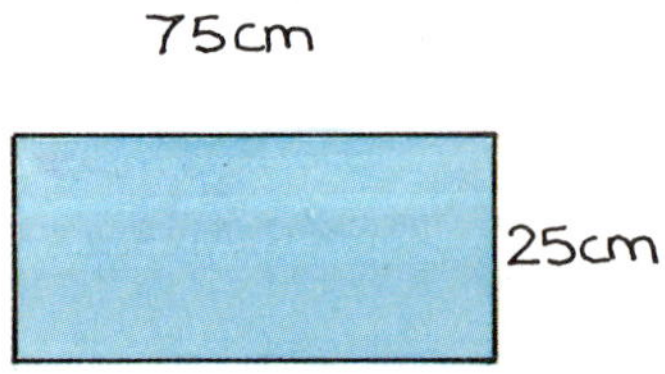

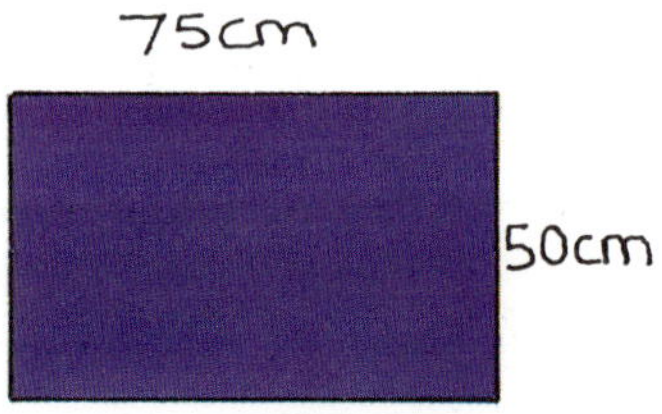

_______ hairy feet   _______ hairy feet   _______ hairy feet

Fractions (2)

$\frac{2}{4}$ of this snake is yellow.

$\frac{1}{2}$ of this snake is yellow.

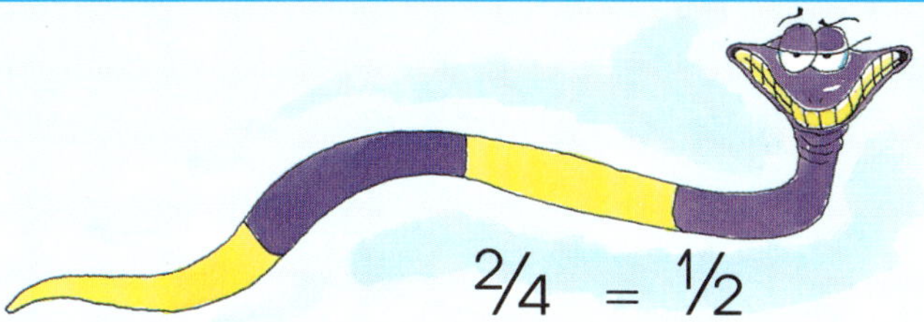

$\frac{2}{4} = \frac{1}{2}$

Use the strips to help you fill in the missing numbers.

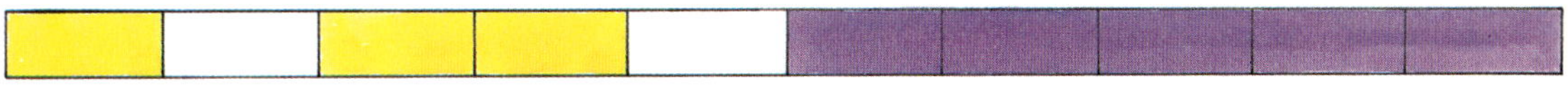

$\frac{1}{10}$ one tenth | $\frac{1}{5}$ one fifth | $\frac{1}{2}$ one half

$\frac{1}{2} = \frac{\square}{10}$ | $\frac{1}{5} = \frac{\square}{10}$ | $\frac{4}{10} = \frac{\square}{5}$ | $\frac{6}{10} = \frac{\square}{5}$

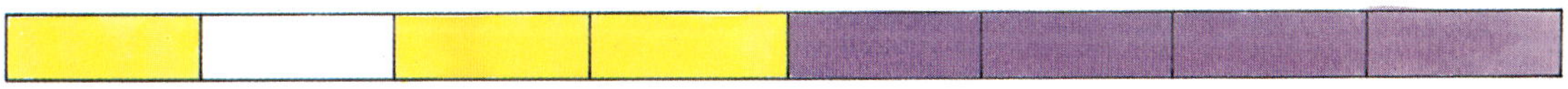

$\frac{1}{8}$ one eighth | $\frac{1}{4}$ one quarter | $\frac{1}{2}$ one half

$\frac{1}{2} = \frac{\square}{4}$ | $\frac{2}{8} = \frac{\square}{4}$ | $\frac{4}{8} = \frac{\square}{2}$ | $\frac{6}{8} = \frac{\square}{4}$

Write down the answers.

$\frac{1}{2}$ of 8 = $\square$	$\frac{1}{2}$ of 6 = $\square$	$\frac{1}{2}$ of 10 = $\square$	$\frac{1}{2}$ of 12 = $\square$
$\frac{1}{3}$ of 3 = $\square$	$\frac{1}{3}$ of 6 = $\square$	$\frac{1}{3}$ of 9 = $\square$	$\frac{1}{3}$ of 12 = $\square$
$\frac{1}{4}$ of 4 = $\square$	$\frac{1}{4}$ of 8 = $\square$	$\frac{1}{4}$ of 12 = $\square$	$\frac{1}{4}$ of 16 = $\square$
$\frac{1}{5}$ of 5 = $\square$	$\frac{1}{5}$ of 10 = $\square$	$\frac{1}{5}$ of 15 = $\square$	$\frac{1}{5}$ of 20 = $\square$

Multiplication (2)

$3 \times 2 \times 5$ can be written as

$3 \times (2 \times 5) = 3 \times 10 = 30$

or

$(3 \times 2) \times 5 = 6 \times 5 = 30$

or

$(3 \times 5) \times 2 = 15 \times 2 = 30$

Complete these multiplications.

$7 \times 2 \times 5$

$7 \times (2 \times 5) = 7 \times \square = \square$

$(7 \times 2) \times 5 = \square \times 5 = \square$

$(7 \times 5) \times 2 = \square \times \square = \square$

$5 \times 4 \times 3$

$5 \times (4 \times 3) = \square \times \square = \square$

$(5 \times 4) \times 3 = \square \times \square = \square$

$(5 \times 3) \times 4 = \square \times \square = \square$

$9 \times 3 \times 5$

$(9 \times 3) \times 5 = \square \times \square = \square$

$9 \times (3 \times 5) = \square \times \square = \square$

$(9 \times 5) \times 3 = \square \times \square = \square$

Multiply each set of numbers together.

5, 2, 7	4, 10, 3	2, 6, 3	5, 3, 6, 10	10, 4, 3, 0	0, 6, 5, 2
5 × 2 × 7	______	______	______	______	______

Answer ______ ______ ______ ______ ______ ______

Length (2)

This bed is 1 metre wide.

1 m = 100 cm

metre ↗ ↖ centimetre

Change these measurements to centimetres.

1 1m = ____ cm	**2** 4m = ____ cm	**3** 10m = ____ cm
4 5m = ____ cm	**5** 3m = ____ cm	**6** 6m = ____ cm
7 ½m = ____ cm	**8** ¼m = ____ cm	**9** ¾m = ____ cm
10 ⅒m = ____ cm	**11** 2½m = ____ cm	**12** 1.2m = ____ cm

Change these measurements to m and cm.

13 120cm = 1 m ____ cm	**14** 199cm = ____ m 99 cm
15 250cm = ____ m ____ cm	**16** 402cm = ____ m ____ cm
17 420cm = ____ m ____ cm	**18** 240cm = ____ m ____ cm
19 353cm = ____ m ____ cm	**20** 172cm = ____ m ____ cm
21 999cm = ____ m ____ cm	**22** 509cm = ____ m ____ cm

Complete these additions.

23

	m	cm
	1	50
+	1	60
		10

24

	m	cm
	2	75
+	3	75

25

	m	cm
	5	39
+	2	61

26 1½m + 50cm = ____ m

27 2m 55cm + 1m 45cm = ____ m

Answers

To Parents:

We have not provided *all* the answers here. We suggest that items to be drawn on clocks, snakes, etc., should be checked by you. In the case of activities where calculations are performed by your child, it would be good practice to get him/her to use a calculator to check the answers.

Page 2

58 ,8 0,766,567
664,655,602,692
798,1000,1313,1000
1171,1332,1000,1099

Page 3

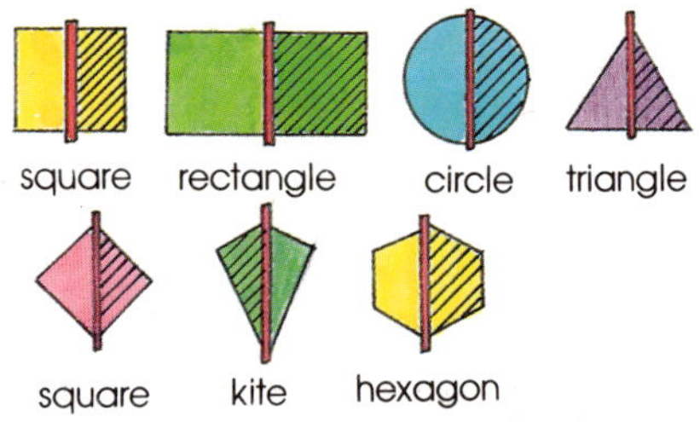

Page 4

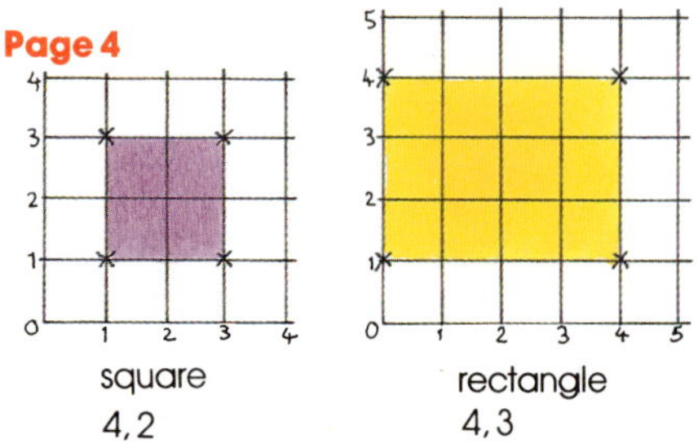

Page 5

10,10
1,25
2, 3
8,20
2, 8
33,0.27
0.11,8
10
Yes

Page 6

16
9

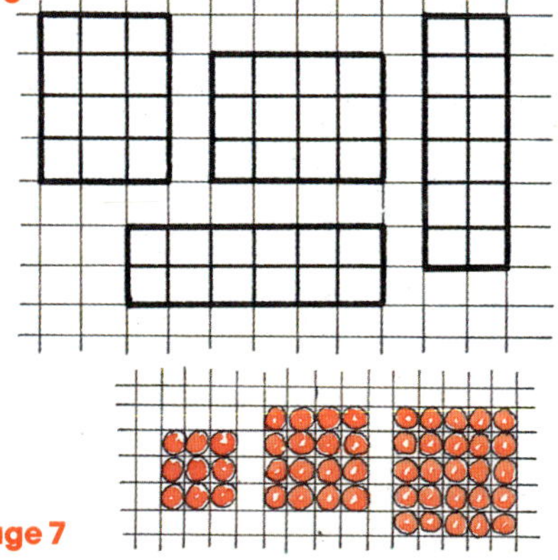

Page 7

111,111,219,190
689,543,172, 99
900,901,909,112
999
900
8 0,0 1,2 2,2

Page 8

2, 3, 3

Page 9

1 343,225,500,60,8
2 547,233,700,70,10,780
3 454,435,800,80,9,889
4 547,232,700,70,9,779
5 245,323,500,60,8,568
6 222,668,800,80,10,890
7 345,345,600,80,10,690
8 436,355,700,80,11,791
9 273,534,700,100,7,807
10 154,254,300,100,8,408
11 495,315,700,100,10,810
12 492,315,700,100,7,807

Page 10

3432
1220
2041
1020

3459,3087,2005,1000
3864,4693,3385,5060

2255,2331

Page 11

0306,0310,0315
1015,1115,0925
0930,0935,0940
0855,1159,1111
0715 0845
650

Page 12

38p, 56p, 62p, 76p, 78p, 99p, 77p
72p, 80p, 80p, 85p, 150p or £1.50,
225p or £2.25

Page 13

卌 卌 II 12 卌 III 8
卌 IIII 9 卌 II 7
IIII 4

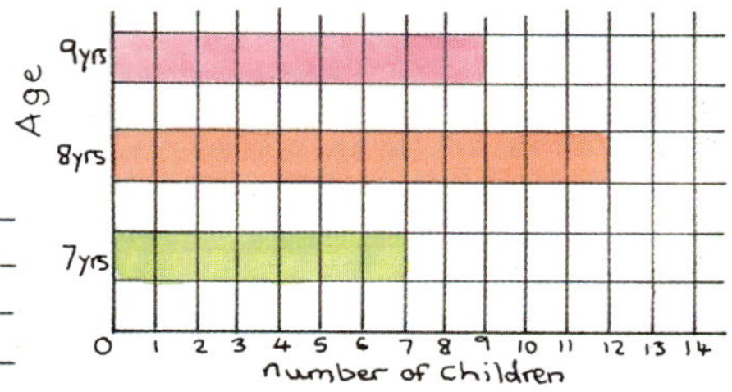

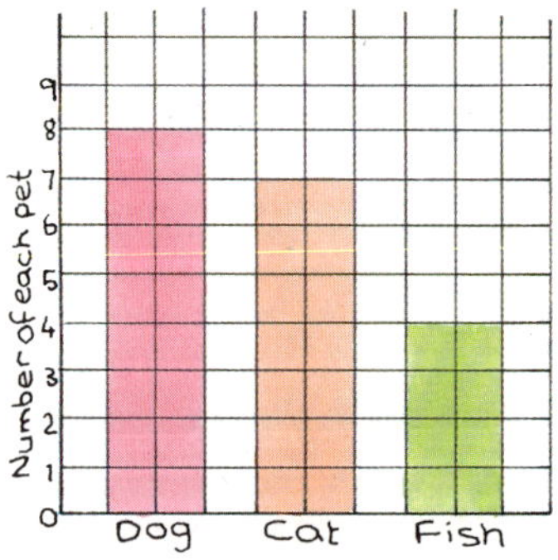

Page 14

15,20 28,35,42 40,45
18,24 32,40,48 48,54

28,32 21,24 20,25 24,30
42,48 35,40 28,35 32,40
56,64 49,56 36,45 40,50

25,35,45 16,24,32 0, 0, 0
35,49,63 24,36,48 0,25,50
45,63,81 32,48,64 0,50,100

5,10,15,20,25 30,35,40,45,50
6,12,18,24,30 36,42,48,54,60
7,14,21,28,35 42,49,56,63,70

Page 15

28
4
February
14
14
A leap year

						Total
Mon	1	8	15	22	–	
Tues	2	9	16	23	–	50
Wed	3	10	17	24	–	
Thurs	4	11	18	25	–	
Fri	5	12	19	26	–	
Sat	6	13	20	27	–	
Sun	7	14	21	28	–	
Totals				175	0	

Page 16

16p:				1	–	1
35p	–	1	1	1	–	–
49p	–	2	–	1	2	–
59p	1	–	–	1	2	–
28p	–	1	–	1	1	1
63p	1	–	1	–	1	1
77p	1	1	–	1	–	1
79p	1	1	–	1	2	–
84p	1	1	1	–	2	–
98p	1	2	–	1	1	1
99p	1	2	–	1	2	–
£1	2	–	–	–	–	–

Page 17

20 to 2, 10 to 2,
2 o'clock, 25 to 2, 5 to 2,
½ past 2, ¼ past 2, 20 past 2
10.20, 2.20, 1.20
9.50, 1.35, 8.50

Page 18

3,2
12,8,4,3
13,9,5,7
17,10,9,9
12,11,17,11
3,3 11,1
16,1 6,1
5,1 10,3
6,1 8,5
7,1 10,1
5

Page 19

5,6,4

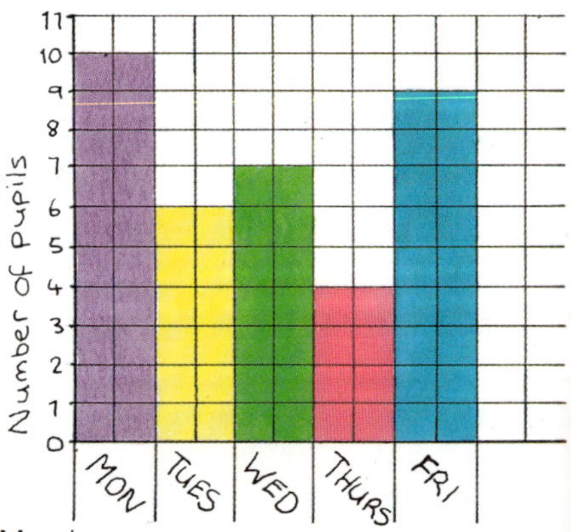

Monday
Thursday
8,5,4
17